Cloudfish
John McCullough

First published October 2007 by

pighog

PO Box 145
Brighton BN1 6YU
UK

info@pighog.co.uk
www.pighog.co.uk

ISBN 0-9542443-7-0

In association with THE SOUTH
www.thesouth.org.uk

Design by Curious
www.curiousdesign.com

Contents

Tropospheric

Clouds know one word and always sing it.
Roughly translated it is *change*
though with inflection it can mean
grow, unite or *decay.* Icebergs puzzle clouds
because they are locked stiff
and cannot join in with air anthems
or life itself which is a wind rolling
through a cloud, shaping its change.

Which is not to say these singers think
their potential for new bodies
is a simple affair; it is uncertain
whether or not the white blobs
glued to hills are changed clouds
playing in a new pitch.

Cloud-sex – or merging and changing –
does not help matters because it makes
it hard to remember who they are
or were. This is why clouds sound a low note
after birds plunge through them:
for that one moment they are distinct.

The alien firmness of those
that share the skyways leads
tragic-minded clouds to lament the bars
which confine them, to believe heaven
is far below and they are in changing hell.
After rain the air is full of such sad ones
left behind to glimpse the souls of the departed
in lakes, rivers and oceans.

Rumour has it one day these dead will return
en masse and the sea will be completely
in the sky for ever, bringing the end
of change as clouds know it
with no more sex and no more songs,
just one big cloud
and one enormous, impossible word.

Spell

This is the hour everything
on the street squeezes into itself,
when walls or a ladder
are on the cusp
before waves sweep in
or the new regime starts.
The one with the trees in charge.

When sun is thrown on a wet road
and you find yourself nodding,
feel your barren mouth opening
for the coins of light,
the lampposts' orange moons
bursting Volvo bonnets.

Leaves are smaller gods now.
And the woman opposite
leaning over a cup
will some day come to own
all she might crave.

Except the field mouse of course,
the one from her dream,
its eager head twisting
through the hedge like *yes*.

Known Light

Now you're crossing that ocean, I have to confess
I've rather warmed to this shed where nothing is yours,
where your father found God in a Bunsen flame.

Chipped oak, a gas tap, scores of powdered specimens –
the perfect stage for resurrecting my A level chemistry.
I remember this much:

a Nichrome wire dipped in compounds then in fire
bares their truer colours.
It's a bit like those stars,

the ones you rehearsed on the pebbles at Kemp Town:
the blood in Betelgeuse, Rigel's furtive blue –
they only show under fiercer, more devoted attention;

you have to *inspire* electrons if you want to unveil
calcium's brick-red, barium's green,
the strange lilac which means simply *potassium.*

Loyal friends, they return now at my diffident prodding,
make me smug as a sorcerer,
impatient for knowledge of the lone unlabelled jar.

Reveal yourself, sweet familiar, I whisper to glass
before I'm blinded by the white heat
of a magnesium heart.

The Loft Fire

I used to wish I'd been there.
Not to rescue the computer,
not to sigh in any undue
affection for shelves
but to rise into the room slowly,
the way I once scaled an oak:
eyes on handholds
till I was enclosed
by a chlorophyll sky
shading spiders and the insects
I never saw but felt waiting.

But when I stood at the foot
of the ladder weeks later
I couldn't think a green thought,
couldn't imagine fire or smoke,
only this: a torrent of moths
swirling down through the hatch
till I was wearing a brown suit,
their papery wings folding
shut cleanly as fans.
A smell of autumn leaves,
warm, rotten and rife.

Riding Back from Highbury

      I've learnt how to spit.
Huffy losers, my brother and me are bumping off linesmen
when this stranger starts sliding his fingers towards
a sleeping girl's bag strap. He closes in with each
lurch of the carriage, eyes fixed on dark tunnel
like this is nothing of his, this crafty hand, this patient spider.
My heart thumps for years but I've staggered five times
before I shove him and apologize: my usual solution.

Or no, that's still not truthful. Swap *fall on* for *shove*
and make that *sorry* unfeigned. The napper's saved by fate
and what scares me isn't louring but the phone call
that hand makes to a black truck in Watford,
the house we'll find is a gap in the street's grin,
a trail of slates and glass decking tarmac like rain.

Reading Frank O'Hara on the Brighton Express

I could believe we are stationary;
it's only everything out there kindly
hurtling past – the grey verticals of Clapham revealed
as bars of a song. I could cock my ear
to catch cirrus chit-chat then touch
down at Gatwick and watch parked cars kiss
in tidy rows. Which reminds me to sort
my manners out, to raise a hand to waving trees
whizzing backwards, plastic bags in their branches
brilliant flags announcing carnivals
in Balcombe, Wivelsfield, Hassocks.

I could trill like a starling myself, bless everything outside
and within this case of human fireworks –
the silver-chained lads probing Burger King bags
like lucky dips; the tannoy woman who is Our Lady, surely,
with a mobile altar of Ribena and Coke;
the suits with *Guardians* hiding *Heat* magazine.

I could realize Brighton doesn't exist,
is being invented for our arrival,
the shops plugged in, the prom laid down,
the smiles carved in random pebbles there
where buses have names so we can
get knocked down by Dusty Springfield.

I could conjure up crowds auditioning for the North Laine –
all dreadlocks and posturing, giros and big schemes
with different kinds of queen walking
different kinds of dog; all the clutter that dashes
or repairs Brighton dreams, that brings gloom or hope
for that pier swaying over the surf.

It all glides on towards Bauble houses
and the united panes of Betjeman's station
though it's not him but you, Frank, that I picture
in the station café, coughing your lungs out
above a latte as you eye up the black waiter.

In just a moment I shall pass the gates
of heaven and find you,
all memories of travel left in the ticket machine
as we stroll out down Queens Road,
the sun on our skin, the sea shining so whitely
that we stop and stare and cannot look away.

Cold Fusion

March thaws the ocean
and I begin spinning pebbles into the shoal.
Speedboats reclaim the lavender distance,
their glittering backwash diminished
in the slap and suck at my feet.

On jetties, men clank huge buckets of mussels,
their rubber soles squelching
past crate stacks, flung rope.
The air stinks of spilt fish guts and petrified jokes:
Husband comes home to find his wife…

Last month, they hoisted a dead man
from the ice's long shadow,
a small crowd of us watching.
Matted hair – blond, his face purple and mustard;
he seemed to be mulling over inscrutable algebra.
The post-mortem will probably show he was drunk.

A passing nurse crossed herself,
two boys dashed for a bus
and I carried on home
trying to skate round your absence.

It's my turn to phone your mother
though I think instead that I'll write:
some cool words telling her everything's fine.

In my recurring dream, I swim instinctively
back to that Christmas
to sweep again all the icicles
from under your bedroom window.

Sagging with Plums

Sunburnt and penniless, your sister ends up working
on a market stall with the uncle
you only mention in corners,
limply stuffing green bananas into paper bags.

Scoured pigs sway on their hooks
in the butcher's opposite, the smell stitched
through her skin when she clumps home,
slides straight into the shower.

Bad enough, friend, but tell me what you say after
she's caught the glint of his scissors
and chopped off her hair in the Ladies,

her fist swinging a blonde rope
when she skips in that evening,
one sleeve sagging with plums.

Foucault's Spoons

Barthes, Genet, Julie Christie: we've kissed them all
but our master's thick lips are still our favourites.

His slow steps create pandemonium in the drawer –
a high-pitched ring fit to splinter a coupe –

till we're dumbstruck when he yanks us
back into the light. Inevitably, he's prepared himself

something astounding, his arguments
for aniseed or lime sanctified by his tongue.

Lying there, we can taste stranger residues:
hash, the tang of semen. It's a spoon's version of heaven;

he'll never guess but we sigh the whole time
as we meet the stiff rubs of the scourer and cloth,

as he nests us precisely on top of each other
and the darkness glides over our heads.

On Galileo's Birthday

I asked and whoops you bought a universe
from B&Q. A bowl of cacti, each one a fat galaxy

of spiny stars. Or are they more specific zodiacs?
Unyielding trio, do they steer our lives like Fates?

I can't remember life without them, imagine if we sifted –
or tried to sift – their sea of granite chips we'd find

only a puzzle of abstract roots, no graspable trace
of what keeps us awake on cold moonless nights,

plotting outer and earthly and inner space.

Sneakers

They invaded Pacific shallows without a sound:
high-tops bob-bobbing from beachcombers' dreams.
Tabloid gold, the storm that jounced their ship,
El Niño that ordered Alaska to *Just Do It*.

Their saviours, air-cushioned soles:
unexpected life jackets that give us hope
though it's the missing I can't forget,
those resolute types that rode foam for weeks,

questing under Sirius and a fairy-tale moon:
swoosh-striped leather Crusoes
I see tumbling across unatlased shores
to reach palm leaves, puffballs, a slow, glorious fade.

A Soupy June

        The sun adrift,
the shoal primeval ooze
spawning life in the half-light.
Condoms like jellyfish, cellophane rays,
the tops of tower blocks bitten off
by a misty Jabberwock.

        But I am a monster too.
I am an addict aching so hard for skin
I'd pull myself through Brighton sewers;
lie, steal or inform on friends if they didn't give me
a wide, sensible berth.

        Like Beardsley,
I see everything in black and white,
everyone as viscous and obvious:
skinheads that belong in masks and frills
beside the Pavilion's eight-breasted cleavage;
amoebic chubbies that reek
of unearthly come.

        I'm so far gone
I see Aubrey on the Palace Pier:
sallow-faced, sunken-eyed
and got up as tarty Salomé, performing
the dance of the seven veils
in the queue for the dodgems.

        My one excuse
is this: that too often I fell asleep on the shore,
that spray deluged my lungs so I woke
with sleaze in my bloodstream, filth
in the cells, my brain only able to muster
salty verbs, unspeakable and churning.

My Bohemia

Freely after Rimbaud

And so I left, fists sunk into the pockets
of a *fleece* stitched together by no more than that word.
Great Muses, I walked chalk paths as your willing slave
and *ah!* what salty dreams were my reward.

My only track suit bottoms had a hole
vast enough to let in Boreas but I didn't
care, sowed rhyme with each step, my motel
The Bulldog, its stars a clutch of queens.

In thickets on cool September nights, I listened
with strangers to rain falling, seeping down
to underground streams or releasing the soil's scents;

and there, hemmed in by bushes, I rhymed
aloud and strummed the laces of my battered pumps
like an acoustic, one foot below my heart.

Downpour on St James Street

feral clouds stealing in from the Downs,
lashing alleys that undress the sea.

Except they don't
when the air's busy; it's rain that captivates
olives like heaped eyes in The Cherry Tree deli,
the clamour absorbed by dried pepper-ears.

It's symbolic,
declares Steve in Clone Zone, *of the internet bringing*
the porn mags to their knees,
wounding favourites like *Hard Ballz* and *Inches*
though the market's still safe
for butt plugs and twinkwear.

But it's macs they need now
on the open-top buses, brollies that are lusted for
by those exiled from salons, pegging their way
past bow-windows and Regency tiles
that hide dodgy plumbing and hangovers
and Big Mike *not taking the pills no more*
cos they was killin' me.

Yes it's pissing it down
on everyone moving out, on hordes heading up north
or to America over the widening ocean
which you can't swim in round here, even in sun,
any more than you can breaststroke in Victoria Fountain,
full already to the brim, yet still receiving so much
that it gleefully gives in
and vanquishes its borders.

Unbreaking a Stone

With you asleep, I sneak downstairs
and pass the night in the company of geodes.
Each has a story, some hollow: a nothingness
I can read the world through. My favourite's
violet and cream: boiled sweet bands
that wall in a crystalline core so furious
it's like looking down on a thunderstorm.

But there was no kind way of bringing it
to this room. It had to be smuggled
out of that river, coaxed open with a hammer.
And let's not pretend the earth doesn't fracture
itself every day, lay bare its heart to send minerals
bubbling up like kisses. Some centres must burst
to make their beauty known.

Like us, reunited after your flight, squeezing
each other's hands on holiday inside a honeycomb
of cool, crumbling limestone we penetrated together:
a Bronze Age labyrinth that smudged
bone tools malachite-green. Those miners craved
the pith of sealed ground too, hauled it up in splinters
to prize it in more generous light.

I steal back to bed, the moonlit embryo of you,
fitting myself against your warm curves
and thinking not of the morning's bright hammer
but a darkness deeper and colder than this,
a river never swum, blacker, more unearthly than Lethe
with winding spectres for fishes
and geodes, blissful geodes, dreaming underneath.

Something Fiercer

Buttons do not enjoy comparisons
with pills or coins.
Those devious tones as they bump
into fingernails, those ticks and clacks
are trademarked in the button world
they inhabit when left
to their own devices.

Nor is it necessary or helpful to assume
buttons are smaller versions of people.
Their lives have different, specific edges.
Consider button art, a set of possibilities
awakened not just by hanging
on shirts but through wheeling
off into collages or assembling in jars.

When buttons meet, a spark
of something fiercer is audible –
halfway between desire
and accepted fate.
That's when a layer melts,
when button games resume,
slow and global and serious.

The Aquarium Party

Octopoda apollyon

Part shaman, all showman, he glides
round his tank in ritual.

The sacred geometry of his web opens
gateways between tentacles allowing the dream

behind the window to inhabit him, to reveal
he is one cell in an ageless octopus.

No sea more real than this, he scrutinizes the kaleidoscope
of himself, discovering and adjusting in response

until, exhausted, he confines himself again,
his three thumping hearts swollen with after-images,

his fungal suckers flattening on glass
the hard-won message, a hundred open eyes.

Lion Fish

Something of the drag queen
in the grand indifference of one
tricked out in zebra print,
a tossed glance disclosing decades
of searing putdowns and pantomime
before the great spiky heart
veers away from your concern.

Conger

You approach like she's a live cable,
a lurker with her crowbar head
and stoned, unanswered eyes
that won't fool you.

Yet a moment later she's a lava lamp's wax,
pure muscular grace as she towers
into a slow, smooth backflip,
returns to meet you, face-on, at the glass.

Stingrays

Bubbly pancakes who satisfy your appetite for friendship.

Seahorse

      Swollen
    daddy-to-be, he
    needs truths to
cling to, metaphysics
      he can coil
      a tail round,
     each vertical
    of coral
    a superstring
      in the radiant
      weave
       where
       his darling
        pearls
      will
     nestle
    and
glimmer.

Dragons

Empty railway carriages
fill our afternoon,

your breath smoky from winter
as you clump through each door.

Your left arm, tattooed,
boasts a red dragon now cooled

to the pink of your lip.
Your grin opens.

Quick eyes,
bare hands on my zip.

Coombeland

Work of the devil. Dark place where hills
mould men. Sense and breath adjust
to a muscular camber, the ground's diaphragm,
small houses riding contractions, stiff verbs.

Chalk ridges give the dialects backbone.
The hole-ridden earth draws in watery vowels.
Ploughshares bring up guttural relics,
flint-teeth with the sibilant ocean inside.

Stroke a nugget of chalk. Already white dust accents
the contours of your fingertips. You inhabit
the past tense, submit to a crumbling tongue

the way the hard *c* in *coombe* yields
to liquid and the unsayable ghost of a *b*
that's the beat of the land's hollow heart.

The Cloud Makers

They played each other at chess,
Zeus and Marduk moving cirri like pawns;
Frigg massing her flocks to trap
the boys in checkmate. Down below
we simply followed one side,
could only guess at the larger game.
A raindancer's honour was dashed or saved
on a whim, the giant hands loitering
before harvest or drought.

Then men flew to heaven.
Balloonists passed out from lack of oxygen,
were felled by gravity. Cloud names shifted
the sky closer, condensed the gods
into ice and water. Only the pieces remained –
Odin's cumulus castles or great teams
of white horses bursting free from their reins.

Now satellites draw nimbi on computer screens.
We use radar to gauge the heart
of a thunderstorm's plan yet we still dream
of makers, some architects behind
these islands or oceans above us
with their promise of change –
wet prophets whispering *rebuild, rebuild again.*

Hyacinths

Don't flatter yourself you came
of your own accord.
This floral horde has opened
for the courting season
and pagan sorcery

ensures you lift each bell,
forces you to skim a finger
down livid green swords
and remember not Tiepolo's wounded boy
but Hyacinth the hunter:

the leopard prince who clutched
his discus with resolve
as well as grace, forever battling
to match a god whose casts
full-rhymed with comets.

These descendents on love's front line
retain his guts, scorn every lesson:
incurable challengers whose shaken blades
would make the sky capsize
just to bring the sun closer.

Apollo transformed blood from his dead lover Hyacinth into the flower that keeps his name.

Motile

What sticks is the hum
of the fridge in your basement,
a plane ticket, trans-Atlantic, lying flat on one chair.
The way, fag in hand, you order me to stop smoking:
you'll damage your cilia

and you conjure those tiny threads stroking together,
pushing wayward particles where they belong.
You drain a glass of vodka,
write my name on the page of your diary
where you wake in a new country.

You keep your promise:
two hours and twenty dollars on a dodgy line
from a city without Marmite
where you tussle with silverfish
and baseball shirt slang.

My cruelly besieged friend,
in these fathomless times
I stroll down to the ocean at night
to set my hand on its skin
and my mind on rowing, rowing, rowing.

The Iceberg Marlene

She who's never been anywhere
without the whole shebang:
kettle drums, entourage, cloak of foam.
Watch her now: a white fortress advancing
to flirt with Arctic mountains,
unscarable as Lola-Lola.
A gorgeous slow-motion river,
each drop *bona fide* stuff you could bottle.

Lean in for the close-up.
Yes, she was lying: she's mere rubble,
devastated like the moon,
her face breaking into a mosaic,
suffocating beneath strata of make-up.
She can't steer herself,
has stared at the sky so long
she thinks she might be a cloud.

She doesn't even know
what's going on in her own body:
lakes swelling inside her,
cruel tunnels opening, collapsing,
cracks burrowing to plunge
her into psychosis.

Or has she fooled you again?
You can never take Marlene seriously
because, as she'd tell you, she's Hollywood
in its enormity, a glassy puzzle
of bit-parts, all waiting
to be applauded by everybody,
each loving the world that much.

Acknowledgements

I would like to thank the editors of the publications in which some of these poems have appeared: *Magma, The Rialto, The Guardian, Smiths Knoll, Reactions, Breach, The New Writer, The Watch List, Chroma, Tall Lighthouse Review, Mean, Erratica*. 'Known Light', 'Sneakers' and 'Reading Frank O'Hara on the Brighton Express' were performed at the *Magma* tenth anniversary celebrations at The Cochrane Theatre, Holborn on January 21 2005.

My thanks go also to those who have read and commented on earlier drafts of my work: Abi Curtis, Ellen de Vries, Maria Jastrzebska, Kate Lyon, Cathy Martin, Neil Martin, John O'Donoghue, Tim Robertson, Catherine Smith, Pauline Suett-Barbieri, Jackie Wills, Gregory Woods, members of Club 94 and the Sussex Writing Group and especially Helen Oswald. I have also benefited greatly from workshops by Don Paterson and Esther Morgan.

This book is dedicated to my partner Morgan Case and my family.